The Book of

NICK POTAMITIS was born i
London. His poetry was short-l
in 2004 and has appeared onlii
and ant

The Book of Night Terrors

by

NICK POTAMITIS

LONDON

PUBLISHED BY SALT PUBLISHING
Dutch House, 307–308 High Holborn, London WC1V 7LL United Kingdom

All rights reserved

© Nick Potamitis, 2010

The right of Nick Potamitis to be identified as the
author of this work has been asserted by him in accordance
with Section 77 of the Copyright, Designs and Patents Act 1988.

This book is in copyright. Subject to statutory exception
and to provisions of relevant collective licensing agreements,
no reproduction of any part may take place without the written
permission of Salt Publishing.

Salt Publishing 2010

Printed in Great Britain by the MPG Books Group, Bodmin and King's Lynn

Typeset in Swift 9.5 / 13

*This book is sold subject to the conditions that it shall not,
by way of trade or otherwise, be lent, re-sold, hired out,
or otherwise circulated without the publisher's prior consent
in any form of binding or cover other than that in which
it is published and without a similar condition including this
condition being imposed on the subsequent purchaser.*

ISBN 978 1 84471 790 3 paperback

1 3 5 7 9 8 6 4 2

For Lenka

Contents

N. 1

nine coffins 25

a book of night terrors 39

Acknowledgements

Earlier versions of these poems were published in pamphlet form by Perdika Press and in *Shearsman Magazine, The Cambridge Literary Review* and in the anthology, *"...further evidence of nerves"*.

The author would like to thank Jon Baines, Rosalind Bouverie, Peter Brennan, Tom Chivers, Alex Davies, Graeme Estry, Helen Ferguson, Tom Jones, Tony Paraskeva, Neil Pattison, Luke Roberts, Peter Stavrou and Steve Willey for their encouragement and opinions.

N.

nontets one to nineteen

I don't understand those big immobile things

— C.P. CAVAFY

ONE

The Capitulation of Arábi Pasha (PART ONE)

       N—— despite hostile declarations
expected still to make an appearance — inflexible —
nuanced trade agreements   brokered by ship-of-the-line
    still no sign of N——   ruddy hundred pounders blast
      escarpments, the minaret of Kait Bey,   others
      might be   working overtime at service-stations
   or checking late editions for tells   eventually amidst muezzin-
      -splattered rubble   he shows   pink, embarrassed
      & not a little   disappointed

TWO

                    Credentials malpronounced by civic
          functionaries   finally we agree upon
superfluous care & a glass of Mother's Ruin — the morning after
    legs fuse   — shorting —   immobile like pylons
      sparked — names now a Turk's dressing-gown
     (something I wear to mask muscles twitching
spasmodic   irreverent   —   like flies to the leanest of horses
       I remember his respite carer was fat & Irish
       as all nurses should be

THREE

                    Swaddled in nervousness & Chiot lace
N— tests his catchpenny inheritance :   electroplated
fob & chain   predisposition to maladies of spirit
  eye for theosophic circuitry   — elsewhere, in the choice
    of seafaring grand-père   genealogists note
    an accord of dynastic urge & ecclesiastic reckoning
so saddled   N— charged — convulsive
    is plugged into blue   patrilineal
    current

FOUR

                    Voltage flares the Arriflex lantern
            sleepy-eyed the septegenarian by noirish lapels
   known,   worked the breweries & the bins,   bruised
by the gendarmerie   incarnation of Saint Moses the
       Ethiopian or bloody-aproned Markos the butcher,
       Assan Bey the car-mechanic — all but Scotch Mick,
  whose absence signifies nothing   but the banal necessity
        of having to re-advertise   — men like these
        might fill an auditorium

FIVE

                   Lento   something suspect about this
        annotated Levant   family romance abstracted from
lithographs — colorized — prosaic begettings, like N——'s
  cheeks,   rouged — chromatypes of the Charing Cross Road
       or the Grande Rue de Pera — curatori of ephemera insist
       we each dream some other architecture anyway
    for N—— a low-coursed wall outside art deco metro
      for his mother   the impromptu proscenia
      of a touring *Blood Wedding*

SIX

The Queen of Spades

                In ribbons and vintage petticoats,
      Niña — prettied — imperilled by wolf & by woodsman
partial to Germans in white socks   six thousand migratory souls
      vying for invitations to tea   N—— of course
      learnéd Herr Falmereyer,   Mistress Burpybeerbelly,
      His August Majesty   the King of Spain
a cosmopolitan and suitably politic imagination   (tho despite
      his being only an archetype, the philologist still
      finds fault with the tableware

SEVEN

His haemorrhaging prick
hurried to the hospital   relentless mother scrubs —
impassive   bed sheets recalling a fearful consummation
— he's tapped some lively claret ! —   in Alex, a short-
-circuiting of allegorical logic sparks the prodigy's
emasculation   where gauze dressing & ice water baths
may inspire belief in metempsychosis   later, she's assured
N— will suffer no future dysfunction   (— mark
this prognosis smacks of malpractice

EIGHT

              As if from a djinn,
   or an atomic serum,   as if from an extra-terrestrial
fragment   dread powers bestowed   — irradiated
   — a terrible unrelenting prescience   too terrible
         even for heroes of illustrated adventures   this
         intimate fallout bleakly cognizant of   dull
conspiratorial intent   (ignorant of political geography
         yet in her protestations   discerning only
         the click of derision

NINE

      Having abandoned alexandrines
    for a thing less overdetermined   left instead
  to clinicians to vaunt the value of such   abnegation —
silence   —   sodomy passed over in the connivances
    of etymologists & sage-drinking aunts
     while   for our hero   daily practice of
Professor Atilla's   five-pound dumbbell exercise,
    ingestion of   genuine malt extract   and
  200mg of venlafaxine hydrochloride

TEN

        Prenticed to a painter of funereal
      portraiture — pigment derived from firing of vinous
   sediment   sending sooty-eyed shopgirls & sour
careerists by N——'s chromatics   turned ;
   laundry bluing to ward malocchio
   and draughtsmanship to a credo of spivvery
  deferred   (yet still   the hoary   homely
   inelegance of youth
   indelible

ELEVEN

        Woman does not exist
      & neither does the Parthenon — both just
    so much madjoun and sweetmeat   symptoms
of an overtaxed apophenic phantasy — this then is how it's best
   in separate booths   (closed circuit confection of onomastic
   impulses   —   trey, seven, ace   zigzagged
galvanic his ideogram relays   stained   the sugary flicker
   of a caryatid   caught
   on corroded   nitrate

TWELVE

    By St. Pancras parish egoistes
      snubbed — combustibility of celluloid yet another
inconvenience to Niña's oneirocritica   —   in corsets
  & in crinolines dizened   declaiming   spoony
  for San Franciscan   non-sequiturs
  — how might she be busied in the Piraeus ?
where the asymmetry of dreams makes impossible
   communion   with this   impeccable
   victoriana

THIRTEEN

        Shot dice in caravanserai from Smyrna
to Sarajevo   our correspondent   now, down on his uppers
then,   upon breasts of doughy   Constantinists
N—'s copy dispatched   irregular   traces
  voltaic the arc   of trade routes
  to Stoke Newington —
in the corner   saloon door of Cypriot wideboy
   dented escaping carabinieri
   across the Essex Road

FOURTEEN

Theatre of Sidon (400 AD)

              Bonnie blue-eyed boy
      in the gods & in the gardens   esteemed
coy crafter of illicit Romaica deemed   not suitable
   for drawing-room oratory   — no, best
    described as   sub-rosa our
     pamphleteer   of the choicest mutual
dissipation   shunned by insipid bishopric
  (shared these odes   to a bare
   reciprocity

FIFTEEN

        Most pleased with the mole-skin
    shako   N— maintains his klephtic bequest
at collegiate & extracurricular offices (unaware of mother's
exhuming & unseasoned consumption of the Captain's
    bones   rustication proceeding finally from
    unseemly   incident in the scriptorium
 ((both pass into the pages of the familial songbook
   with N— assuming consequence
   for this   thyroidal ossuary

SIXTEEN

        Amphorae set pyramiding
    to savvy   of Ephesian stevedores
  describing perhaps   circumference of anxiety   unspoken
(should at least secure commission in wartime intelligence
    — this from first principles   supposed
    else   a priapic   compass-wielding deus
sure to topple the Gorgopotamos bridge   ((line being only
    breadthless length   & love derailed
    sending shards in virgin oil   adrift

SEVENTEEN

       Fear of Albanian gangsterism
           decocted through nightly sweats & other assorted
      symptoma of disquiet   — equally extortionate
mine a wormy dam   dunning along   dromoi
    unsafe even for male pedestrians,   summoned
   I call   before the beak unkempt   peevish
as the Stamboul train whose Byzantine terms of carriage
     might clue this mumbled dread
     of maternal cozenage

EIGHTEEN

The Capitulation of Arábi Pasha (PART TWO)

              Heeding domestic obligation
      reluctant to calendrical time   N— bends
    a knee   (tho digestive contra-indications
  veto agrarianism   decided a clerical post might suit
    ((one amongst mythopeia of naval dominance
      another might be the obscurantism of university presses
curmudgeonly as a Myrmidon   N— is duly dismissed
      having shat in his own
      inkstand

NINETEEN

The Capitulation of Arábi Pasha (PART THREE)

                      What conspiracy of planets
    brings the fleet   to these Ptolemaic inlets ?
     salvos saturnine   batter frontages of   shopping arcades
(as tho to some Marxian protocol attended by   hydration
     of sulphur   N—— full of stomach ((dispraising
      his self-willed insensibility   unhears last report
— postbellum our boy'll need a company of well-drilled zouaves
      & plenty of Jeyes' fluid
       — that much is certain

nine coffins

a masque for nectanebo

for the skeptic there remains only one consolation: if there should be such a thing as superhuman law it is administered with subhuman inefficiency

— ERIC AMBLER

ONE

a poem, abstract'd from the royal bedroom

is more, perhaps, than blowsy tsifteteli, or
razor'd statements filling green refuse-sacks

by the road . with these computers can make

an assemblage . behold, a pale dust-cart
bent on waking the dead & neither must you
write down your mother's maidenhood,

the din / such delicate matter . those clamorous

bin-jockeys up at dawn to claim our midden-
heaps — a blight'd wreath — that rowdy
parataxis . by hand, re-program'd refuseniks
will need a bit under six-hundred years

doing the job (for chri'sakes) it's damn
too early for that racket, pantokratoras .

TWO

careening past brassy roma at the platform,

your man & his massive sunglasses disappear
beneath the train . the marble king is asleep .

the man with sunglasses might be an actor

in the part of man falling under a train,
a necessary geometry of position . no one
ever dies, everyone is always already dead,

the tally—on war footing ready to mobilise

—is zero, zero, one & still the marble king
sleeps . that same man, haul'd so many yards,
now a human accordion, his moody pass-
port reads bricoleur balkan nektanebos (

an outstretch'd hand / the sleeping stones
) give them a turn on your squeezebox .

THREE

nightmare outbreak of violent chicken's disease

with pictures . nightmare cowl'd gangs
in the forecourt are a real nightmare, a not

very dada suicide on the metro . consider,

how she loves muscley arms, stakes out—
for future reference—her cleo from five till
seven bed-chamber, wounding & immaculate

as the wings of swans . indifferent, the swan

is a presence in the poem even if poland makes
more ready for nightmare war (one shorn
clean at the shoulder joint / parts of shoulder
bone scatter'd recalling tube mice) & always

on a promise, she would let him only when
he wore that nightmarish ram's head mask .

FOUR

bandwidth & roving 'gyptians are stain'd by grief

the same as linen garments—damn'd / the damages
—his meat thought at no loss, with neat hand only

. things fit together . a basement gallery-space

if she can get away, mojitos, talk of graffiti-
inflect'd art well-hung . two inconsequential
things will fit together, become a consequence

(cropping his beard, his head shaven) mis-

taking her & by her mistaken . as ever, with all
eastern warfare, when the king retreats the buffer
overflows collapsing memory stacks . like small
wax ships on a bronze basin of rain-water,

a poem says jack, is never by itself alone . time
is a concrete continuum quotes jill, in repose .

FIVE

theft is always analogous to mathematical

procedures . there are always remainders .
inspector n.tannenbaum's roving warrant

from pelusium to macedonian pella via the rail-
ways' police semantic web . what's left is the
set of these good / bad objects, the queen —
her sick body — mendoza the jew's bent elbow

& that schoolboy winning every marble .

a function, mon cher juve, of the man vaulting
an automatic ticket barrier . a secret platonic
dossier probably does exist . well-order'd,
it consists of statements given (in a dream

about warring factions) my arms are lost —
they approach me — this fast-track truncation .

SIX

the perseverance of birds over the mountain,

of the poem-computer's royally amorous intrusion .
topology tells us, each element is an equivalence,

symbolic—mostly of real hurt—somewhere

between gods & butchers . the elements being
grammatically uncertain (this ill-conditioning)
precarious as rum nizhinsky resonant with threat

. let the burn mark on her wrist serve for the real

ryght-arm'd in heart, he did hym downe to the
dytch—knock'd spark-out for filching documenta,
or haw-hawing the wrong faces . other versions
have the poem-computer for pseudo-callisthenes

—that need to provoke a stupid embroilment
again—so much ache / so much belly-aching .

SEVEN

a zakopane night-train & from the bottle

niña drinking her home-brought bulgarian
red . niña is a character in a different poem .
more healthy than gin, she stands here for

amplification / for generic processes &
previous war damage . a footnote is a footnote
is a fat clever crow sings jon in warszawa,

gamely wearing his song & dance-man's hat

. niña is (not) that balkan starlet famously
a young royal in dupin contra fantômas .
let's say — by affective peer-review — she
really does marry assistant conductor witold

nectanebosz, falling hard in a stand-up row
over corkage . let's say there are resonances .

EIGHT

the angel of silence taken wing . rouse

yourself old man, wake-up, go tell them
you play the better violin . ravens are military

spy-planes, would say a poem should be a lusty
noise, must croak like a frog smoking dog-ends .
& truly, he is not yet risen — strategically —
his word lent support by that wide-awake

suit, dapper log-book of his observances (with-

out interpretation) no space here for proper
french manners, just reconnoitring . the angel
having flown, leaves birds to pry, left our
lady's creaky ikon . rouse-up, king of the rom

& remember, beneath her vestments a large
candle she raises / it went aflame .

NINE

would you hit a woman with a child ? vulture-

wing'd like a polish lancer, return'd general
james & a makriyanni shoe-black barrack'd

as one by ox-flaying sleet — her split plastic bag

— all elements of the set of disavow'd elements .
the poem-computer is not for conflict resolution,
nor is zeus-under-the-ground, suffers phlegm

& the consequences of phlegm, us (the lost ones

) unwrit in the catalogue of the world, spilling
discount'd viscera & only our impotent
inspector — toothless chewer of corpses — to
clutch an exhibition fighter's plaster arm & cuff

copper-bound nectanebo's fallen limb / a lap-
top / the poem, singing not me, i'd use a brick .

a book of night terrors

thirteen variations on a theme

the terrors of the night,
they are as many as our sins

— THOMAS NASHE

ONE

old age

amassing books in expectation
of snow you begin
slowly to take on a patchy
purple colour suggestive of
bomb damage—a blockage
—something not
right in the bones of it

the snow bides & back'd up
by timidity or pride you realign
each volume of patristic
table-talk a batter'd but liveable
shelter for your costive
imagination

nothing shifts beyond
the charr'd blast pattern—
antique shrapnel wounds
—wolves snide & watchful
stalk your reading
& you go slower still
from purple to rust

all else bleakly
stalls

TWO

bleeding

there was no blood on
the mouse corpse you found in
the off-scourings by the kerb

the mouse dying
of grief or heartbreak
in your jacket pocket
it wants only saintliness
to disentangle from
bluebottles & all your
broken theories of mind
or mindfulness

despite the flies
the mouse could have had
no blood in it—only
rosewater—if you cut
your wrist asks the novice of
the nightclub singer will it not
drip wet & cold & clear

is that not what those
sloganeers might & yet
despite their buzzing
wall writings you have us
each redeeming flies turning
our chequer'd tailoring into desert
caves for long tail'd contemplatives

the rest is
commentary

THREE

execution

in one photo
you are wrestling a bull
in lima
& you will
embody each of those vigorous
labours in classical tableaux
whilst on tour

in a second you are just
a giant torso—your tie
that sweater & the check
of your sports coat lapel
filling the frame—
square as a nazirite
—off to the
side & out
of focus thanks to
that giant that insistent
lapel a woman
in pearls you might call
blowsy had you ever
actually learnt some
english – call it
clacton 1963

in the last you are
a digital reproduction of
the fresco of saint raphael
bound to a tree your jawbone
saw'd through by the turk

FOUR

found dead in the streets

it was you on the kerb
bloodless defunct &
splay'd in piss sodden
trews amongst the sweepings
the hybrid chatter
broken clay

your saintly blue
hand on your long-neck'd
saz no longer unpicking
the hazard memory
three courses of strings
& the seraphim's three
pairs of broken wings

bust'd contingencies
that make the host
culture buzz it's all
just greek kids trying to chat like
they were armenians & this
is your one regret o good & over-
seeing angel of disambiguation

that we are
all ultramodernes

FIVE

grief

most people wake
up most days but some
don't—pitch & oil—
a brigade of babushkas
soiling the cobbles &
what's left of that stolen
jacket you always wore

their gums pubic hair
like other stigmatising
prejudices from the old
country function
ritually & everything
goes blackish or slightly
tacky like that folksy
entrepreneurism you could
never convince anyone
to take a punt on

tears & prayer-ropes
regurgitating chew'd & stale
crusts these old women
moulding doughy replicas of
your face weaving moustaches

from their privates & equally
combustible wax paper
cigarettes for your lips of bread

& you will mourn the separation
crying over these death masks
even more for the oily
residue that stains

six

kill'd by various accidents

jump-cut past cockroach
undercarriage under green
rubber sole furiously
reach down & ask
questions of it

this is not an extreme
close up—much
better to use a bigger
typeface or progressively
larger eyeballs to connote
proximity or your skew'd
vantage

not from the cockroach's
gloamy & up-end'd point of view
nor your bedside reading lamp
glamourising spoilage
ask again—
flicker aghast
—carapace heavy with
still smaller cockroaches
spooling & this

is actually quite like your
wedding photo but not
your wedding photo—the people
shorter with different colour'd
eyes—plus the frame
was more rococo

if only you weren't
so shut in by your idiolect
& if not a cockroach
then a dung beetle

in the end a faint
outline persists around everything

SEVEN

lethargy

that winter past you &
your brother playing
brothers—fifteen false
aspirations to fraternity
—like the snow that there is
none of only a tedious
sleet through which the saints
trawl disinterr'd
fractious from their tombs

yet the game's strangely
civilizing unloose from
the nearness of self
regard & slack knee'd
dogs—half
unfinish'd & useless
front—play instead

at being yourself
isolate your nerve & ribs
enlarge vastly an eye
catching detail like the mouths
of dogs wide open—the

ottoman empire—or a snow
crystal cut from the book
of factions

the term book like brothers
or snow crystal is a loanword
from some other idiom
of equally uncertain manoeuvre
ask what synchronises
these six fold symmetries
before they come for their words
back & the dead—
damp & chill'd—return
from jerusalem where they

could not find what they were
looking for

EIGHT

mother

you attach to this title
the image of a madman who
for entertainment summons
his prostrate courtesans
to a riot of genuflexion

& you disown detest protest
this pseudo-orientalism preferring
white-wash'd nostalgia
guilt—retro classic to peck
market-stall colleen
—so what if you had
pollens & pomegranate seeds
blown into your sleeping mouth what
is this menstruous self pitying

try politesse—whispers the doxy
to the deacon—rivers
& sewage sluices run
into the same sea

niña piggyback on your gianelli
scooter her pearls & courgettes
in a brown sack
bouncing behind you

NINE

plague

if not a cockroach or a dung
beetle it must have been
a ladybird land'd on your silk
hatband unperturb'd you
tell of a middle ranking functionary
who order'd an infamous raid
on a bouzouki joint
of a drunken patron
that kill'd a policeman
& his awaiting execution

following the collapse
of the regime the official found
himself bound over—by a people's
tribunal—& in the same cell
as the condemn'd customer

the two have since
become lovers

is that what you call
a parable chides our lady of
the immaculate twinset

is that what you
call charity

TEN

poison

biologically alive
you are telling lies
about how influence
persists about
the significance of that
buzzing sound
so far beyond any
communicable embarrassment

—fatal non-conductor
call it face ache or
spleen—such odd
correspondences of cruelty
an excess of carrier bags
& bluebottles become
defining features of your deconnect'd
sacramental network

yet you cannot die
if you are already dead
like gnostic deadwood from
the life of the proto-martyr—

hurt lingers in the gutter
remembrance fearful others
may claim your one
captive fly mend & make
do the only
antidote

ELEVEN

suddenly

all creatures
exist in your pocket

pulling the ladder behind you
you read you can become
a saint only after death — the other
rule being what happens
in hagia sophia stays in
hagia sophia

you can only really tend
towards sainthood like you
might tend towards off colour
remarks about that perishing
sheet-metal in your bowel

think of the devils
harrying the line
of escalating hermits
batwing'd monkeys who in turn
recall in vest & fez
the chivvying jannisaries of your
sawtooth'd chelsea smile

this communion of saintly
beasts exists in your pocket
& you you are thrice
-bless'd to have been
ditch'd at speed & not
blown utterly disaggregate in
the spray like the rest
of the malaugurati

TWELVE

vomiting

books collapse upon
other books
on the altar table of your
autoscopic devotions—enlighten'd
illiterate—your good
words scatter'd in the mass made
glosses of the herculean
back catalogue they have
titles such as
maciste versus the literalists
while the little icons
point to some raw
& obscure rite

anxious not to
fall prisoner
to any provisional
sect you appropriate
a fur trim'd shapka
to ward against threatening
snow

flies cold &
depart'd litter
the fallen books

& if there was no blood
on the mouse corpse
the dishevell'd altar table
is dark with blood-rich
bat spew

vital &
ferocious filth
without place
without
exception

THIRTEEN

wolf

too much noise
poor niña cries the hounds
abounding seize their prey

they spin & will
no one answer for this
facsimile mise-en-scène —
hierarchies of the disconsolate
blunt & ghost'd —
an overlay'd snapshot
of what's beneath
only slightly to the left
all sides guilty of a grainy
excess

circles of interlocking
bodies revolve about your off-white
corpse & everything of use
in the commerce of graft
an equivalence
in the commerce of grace

it starts to snow
& each gyrate formation
makes a linkage
your blue hand outstretch'd
for the broken neck of your saz
bisecting the scatter radius

flickering your other
hand—reality's
grey cousin—pinch'd in your
pocket heavy with
hatching larvae

too much noise
there is too much
of everything

will it settle

Part family romance, part archive of lost film, part experimental joke-book, this collection brings together for the first time Nick Potamitis' three semi-autobiographical serial poems, written between 2004 and 2009. First published in pamphlet form and small press magazines, these playful, painful sequences explore the interweaving legacies of personal and cultural history, the two forever running at different speeds on the same projector.

"A poetry for those who delight in linguistic fireworks, dizzy-making holes in the path. Mastery of the recherché word. You don't believe they exist but they do, they're history. Keep your Google by your side and you'll be all right." —PETER RILEY

"Full of surprising jags, like a boxful of polystyrene chips packed out with bone china for maximum transit damage." —CHRIS GOODE

NICK POTAMITIS was born in 1975 and grew up in North London. His poetry was shortlisted for an Eric Gregory Award in 2004 and has appeared online and in small press magazines and anthologies.

Cover design by **The Cover Factory**
Cover illustration © Stereohype 2008

http://www.saltpublishing.com